A Special Gift

For

Lorianne Tenove

From

Julie MacInnis

Date

April 1, 2000

Joined at the Heart

What greater earthly good is there
for two human souls, than to feel
that they are joined for life?

~GEORGE ELIOT

You Can Be Yourself

A friend is a person with whom you dare to be yourself. Your soul can go naked with her. She seems to ask of you that you put on nothing, only to be what you are. She does not want you to be better or worse.

When you are with her you feel as a prisoner feels who has been declared innocent. You do not have to be on your guard. You can say what you think so long as it is genuinely you. She understands those contradictions in your nature that lead others to misjudge you.

With her you breathe free. You can take off your shoes and loosen your belt. You can avow your little vanities and envies and hates and vicious sparks, your meanness and absurdities,

and in opening them up to her they are lost, dissolved on the white ocean of her loyalties. She understands. You do not have to be careful.

You can abuse her, neglect her, tolerate her. Best of all, you can keep still with her. It makes no matter. She is like fire that purges all you do. She is like water that cleanses all that you say. She is like wine that warms you to the bone. She understands.

You can weep with her, laugh with her, pray with her. Through and underneath it all she sees, knows, and loves you.

A friend is one with whom you dare to be yourself.

~Author Unknown

More Than a Pleasant Companion

We use the word friend very lightly. We talk of our "host of friends," meaning all with whom we have friendly relations, or even pleasant acquaintance. We say a person is our friend when we know her only in business or socially, when her heart and ours have never touched in any real communion.

To become another's friend in the true sense is to take the other into such close, living fellowship, that her life and ours are knit together as one. It is far more than a pleasant companionship in bright, sunny hours. A true friendship is entirely unselfish. It loves not for what it may receive, but what it may give. Its aim is "not to be ministered unto, but to minister."

It is a sacred thing, therefore, to take a new friend into our life and we accept a solemn responsibility when we do so. We should choose our friends thoughtfully, wisely, prayerfully; but when we have pledged our lives we should be faithful whatever the cost may be.

-J. R. M.

Kind words are the music of the world. They have power that seems to be beyond natural causes, as if they were some angel's song that had lost its way and come on earth.

FREDERICK WILLIAM FABER

Every morning lean thine arms awhile
Upon the window still of heaven
And gaze upon thy Lord.
Then, with the vision in thy heart,
Turn strong to meet thy day.
~AUTHOR UNKNOWN

A friendship that makes the least noise
is very often the most useful; for which
reason I should prefer a prudent friend
to a zealous one.
~ADDISON

What, then, is the true way of loving
one's friends? It is to love them in God,
to love God in them; to love what He has
made them; and to bear for love of Him
what He has not made.
~FENELON

A Quiet Friendship

But, after all, the very best thing in good
talk, and the thing that helps it most, is
friendship. Now it dissolves the barriers
that divide us, and loosens all constraint,
and diffuses itself like some fine old
cordial through all the veins of life. It
transforms letter writing from a task
into a pleasure. It makes music a thou-
sand times more sweet. Yes, there is a
talkability that can express itself even
without words. There is an exchange of
thought and feeling which is happy alike
in speech and in silence. It is quietness
pervaded with friendship.
~HENRY VAN DYKE

Where your pleasure is, there is your treasure. Where your treasure is, there is your heart. Where your heart is, there is your happiness.

~AUGUSTINE

There is no feeling in a human heart that exists in that heart alone—which is not, in some form or degree, in every heart.

~GEORGE MACDONALD

What the heart has once owned and had, it shall never lose.

~HENRY WARD BEECHER

There never was any heart truly great and generous, that was not also tender and compassionate.

~ROBERT FROST

Trust in the Lord with all your heart and lean not on your own understanding; in all your ways acknowledge him and he will make your paths straight.

~PROVERBS 3:5,6

If instead of a gem, or even a flower, we should cast the gift of a loving thought into the heart of a friend, that would be giving as the angels give.

~GEORGE MACDONALD

The dedicated life is the life worth living. You must give with your whole heart.

~ANNIE DILLARD

The human heart yearns for the beautiful in all ranks of life.

~HARRIET BEECHER STOWE

Cultivate the friendly spirit If we would have friends we must be worthy of them. Learn to love; get the helpful spirit, and above all the responsive temper, and friends will come to you as birds fly to their beautiful singing mates.

~T. T. Munger

Within the deeps of her dear eyes
The spirit of the sunshine lies,
And when she turns their light on me,
The shadows of a lifetime flee.
Spring, joy, and love become my part,
For she is sunshine in my heart.

~Lydia Avery Coonley

To the attentive eye, each moment of the year has its own beauty, and in the same field, it beholds every hour, a picture which was never seen before, and which shall never be seen again.

~Ralph Waldo Emerson

It is good to have a friend, but it is better to be a friend. The benefit of being unselfishly loved and sympathized with and cheered and helped, is nothing compared with the joy of unselfishly loving and sympathizing with and helping and cheering another. No amount of love from another's heart can uplift and enlarge like the expansive force of generous and self-forgetting love, working outward from within.

~Anonymous

Love is a tender plant; when properly nourished, it becomes sturdy and enduring, but neglected it will soon wither and die.

~Hugh B. Brown

Whatever may lie beyond us,
The lesson this earth has to give
Is, learn how to love divinely,
And then you have learned
to live.

~Anonymous

A friend is one to whom one may pour out all the contents of one's heart, chaff and grain together, knowing that the gentlest of hands will take and sift it, keep what is worth keeping, and with a breath of kindness, blow the rest away.

~ANONYMOUS

There are great human needs which money has no power to satisfy, but to which a little heart's gentle love will be the very bread of God. There are sorrows money cannot soothe, but which a word of loving comfort will change into songs. The abundant life may not have money to give, and yet it may fill a wide community with blessings. It may go out with sympathy, with comfort, with inspirations of cheer and hope, and may make countless hearts braver and stronger.

~J. R. MILLER

Silver & Gold

Make new friends, but keep the old:
Those that are silver, these are gold.
New-made friendships, like new wine,
Age will mellow and refine.

Friendships that have stood the test~
Time and change~are surely best;
Brow may wrinkle, hair grow gray;
Friendship never knows decay.

Cherish friendship in your breast~
New is good, but old is best;
Make new friends, but keep the old:
Those are silver, these are gold.

~UNKNOWN

Forever Friends

You're the one friend I could count on
when times were not the best.
You're the one who stood by my side
and gave my heart its rest.
And you're the one I've laughed with
when something funny happened
through the years. You're the one
friend who shares with me both
laughter and tears. I think you're
the finest friend there has ever been~
that's why I call you my
forever friend.

ANONYMOUS

The happiest moments my heart knows
are those in which it is pouring forth its
affections to a few esteemed characters.
~THOMAS JEFFERSON

A gentle word, like summer rain,
May soothe some heart and banish pain.
What joy or sadness often springs
From just the simple little things!
~WILLA HOEY

Blessed is the man who has the gift of
making friends: for it is one of God's best
gifts. It involves many things, but above all
the power of going out of one's own self
and seeing and appreciating whatever is
noble and loving in another man.
~THOMAS HUGHES

A Houseful of Heaven

"Oh, how delightful it would be
to live in a house where everybody understood,
and loved, and thought about everybody else!"
She did not know that she was wishing
for nothing more and something a little
less than the kingdom of heaven.

GEORGE MACDONALD

I Shall Not Live In Vain

If I can stop one heart from breaking,

I shall not live in vain;

If I can ease one life the aching,

Or cool one pain,

Or help one fainting robin

Into his nest again,

I shall not live in vain.

EMILY ELIZABETH DICKENSON

© Debbie Mumm

BACKYARD BIRDHOUSES

© Debbie Mumm

Greta

The Garden Angel

Garden Angel

come below.

Warm

and bless

these seeds

I sow.

♥

SEEDS

SEEDS

© Debbie Mumm

The Everyday Angel

For a good everyday household angel give us the woman who laughs. Her pastry may not always be just right, and she may occasionally burn her bread and forget to replace missing buttons, but for solid comfort all day and every day she is an absolute delight. Home is not a battlefield, nor life one long, unending fight. The trick of always seeing the bright side, or, if the matter has no bright side, of polishing up the dark one, is a very important faculty, one of the things no woman should be without. We are not all born with brilliant sun~ shine in our hearts, but we can cultivate a cheerful sense of humor if we only try.

FROM AN OLD SCRAPBOOK

A Beloved Friend

A beloved friend does not fill one part of the soul, but, penetrating the whole, becomes connected with all feeling.

A friend is he who sets his heart upon us, is happy with us, and delights in us; does for us what we want, is willing and fully engaged to do all he can for us, on whom we can rely in all cases.

A true friend embraces our objects as his own. We feel another mind bent on the same end, enjoying it, ensuring it, reflecting it, and delighting in our devotion to it.

Other blessings may be taken away, but if we have acquired a good friend by goodness, we have a blessing which improves in value when others fail. It is even heightened by sufferings.

To be only an admirer is not to be a friend of a human being. Human nature wants something more, and our perceptions are diseased when we dress up a human being in the attributes of divinity. He is our friend who loves more than admires us, and would aid us in our great work.

WILLIAM ELLERY CHANNING

I'm glad the sky is painted blue
And the earth is painted green
With such a lot of nice fresh air
All sandwiched in~between.
~ANONYMOUS

The lives that make the world so sweet
Are shy, and hide like humble flowers;
We pass them by with our careless feet,
Nor dream 'tis their fragrance
    fills the bower,
And cheers and comforts us,
    hour by hour.
~ANONYMOUS

The man who has planted a garden
feels that he has done something for the
good of the whole world.
~CHARLES DUDLEY WARNER

God almighty first planted a garden.
And, indeed, it is the purest of
human pleasures.
~FRANCIS BACON

We all belong to each other, but friendship
is the special connection of one life with a
kindred life. It is harmony felt at the foun~
dations of conscious being, not obliterating
personal differences, but so pervading both
natures as to help each to a happier and
truer expression of itself. It is not that
they seek each the other, but that God
sends each to the other,
because they
belong
together.
~LUCY
LARCOM

True friendship is a knot which angel hands have tied.

~ANTIQUE SAMPLER

The human soul is a silent harp in God's choir, whose strings need only to be swept by the divine breath to chime in with the harmonies of creation.

~HENRY DAVID THOREAU

Friendship cannot be permanent unless it becomes spiritual. There must be fellowship in the deepest things of the soul, community in the highest thoughts, sympathy with the best endeavor.

~HUGH BLACK

The desire for friendship is strong in every human heart. We crave the companionship of those who understand.

~ELBERT HUBBARD

A soul friend is someone with whom we can share our greatest joys and deepest fears, confess our worst sins and most persistent faults, clarify our highest hopes and perhaps most unarticulated dreams.

~EDWARD C. SELLNER

Many there be who call themselves our friends;
Yes, but if heaven sends
One, only one, so mated to our soul,
To make our half a whole,
Rich beyond price are we.

~ANONYMOUS

The course of human history is determined, not by what happens in the skies, but by what takes place in our hearts.

~SIR ARTHUR KEITH

Our friends see the best in us, and by that very fact call forth the best from us.

~HUGH BLACK

Talk not of wasted affection, affection never was wasted.
If it enrich not the heart of another, its waters, returning back to their springs, like the rain, shall fill them full of refreshment. That which the fountain sends forth returns again to the fountain.

HENRY WADSWORTH LONGFELLOW

Watermelon Miracles

I have observed the power of the watermelon seed. It has the power of drawing from the ground and through itself 200,000 times its weight. When you can tell me how it takes this material and out of it colors an outside surface beyond the imitation of art, and then forms inside of it a white rind and within that again a red heart, thickly inlaid with black seeds, each one of which in turn is capable of drawing through itself 200,000 times its weight—when you can explain to me the mystery of a watermelon, you can ask me to explain the mystery of God.

WILLIAM JENNINGS BRYAN

©DEBBIE MUMM

The Simple Pleasures of Life

The happiness of life is made up of minute fractions—the little soon forgotten charities of a kiss or smile, a kind look, a heartfelt compliment, and the countless infinitesimals of pleasurable and genial feeling.

~SAMUEL TAYLOR COLERIDGE

Cheerfulness keeps up a kind of daylight in the mind and fills it with a steady and perpetual serenity.

~JOSEPH ADDISON

Everything true and great grows in silence. Without silence we fall short of reality and cannot plumb the depths of being.

~LADISLAUS BOROS

Happiness is like a potato salad—when shared with others it's a picnic.

~ANONYMOUS

The whole secret of the study of Nature lies in learning to use one's eyes.

~GEORGE SAND

The art of being happy is the art of discovering the depths that lie in the common daily things.

~BRIERLEY

Those who dwell among the beauties and mysteries of the earth are never alone or weary of life.

~RACHEL CARSON

Hurt not the earth, neither the sea, nor the trees.

~REVELATION 7:3

There is much satisfaction in work well done; praise is sweet, but there can be no happiness equal to the joy of finding a heart that understands.

~VICTOR ROBINSOLL

Looking for the Best

One of the greatest lessons in life is to learn to take people at their best, not their worst; to look for the divine, not the human, in them; the beautiful, not the ugly; the bright, not the dark; the straight, not the crooked side.

A habit of looking for the best in everybody, and of saying kindly instead of unkindly things about them, strengthens the character, elevates the ideals, and tends to produce happiness. It also helps to create friends. We like to be with those who see the divine side of us, who see our possibilities, who do not dwell upon the dark side of our life, but upon the bright side. This is the office of a true friend, to help us discover our noblest selves.

~ANONYMOUS

There was a definite process by which one made people into friends, and it involved talking to them and listening to them for hours at a time.
~REBECCA WEST

It is very good for strength,
To know that some one needs you
to be strong.
~ELIZABETH BARRETT BROWNING

Poor indeed is the garden in which birds find no homes.
~ABRAM LINWOOD URBAN

To know of someone here and there whom we accord with, who is living on with us, even in silence~this makes our earthly ball a peopled garden.
~WOLFGANG VON GOETHE

So deeply is the gardener's instinct implanted
in my soul, I really love the tools with which
I work—the iron fork, the spade, the hoe,
the rake, the trowel, and the watering-pot
are pleasant objects in my eyes.
    ~Celia Thaxter

As I work among my flowers,
I find myself talking to them,
reasoning and remonstrating with
them, and adoring them as if they
were human beings. We are on such
good terms, my flowers and I.
~CELIA THAXTER

There are souls in the world who
have the gift of finding joy everywhere
and of leaving it behind them when
they go. Joy gushes under their fingers
like jets of light. Their influence is an
inevitable gladdening of the heart. It
seems as if a shadow of God's own gift
had passed upon them. They give light
without meaning to shine.
~F. W. FABER

Whatever we see, wherever we look,
whether we recognize it as true or not,
we cannot touch or handle the things of
earth and not, in that very moment, be
confronted with the sacraments of heaven.
~C. A. COULSON

Morning is the best of all times
in the garden. The sun is not yet hot.
Sweet vapors rise from the earth.
Night dew clings to the soil and
makes plants glisten. Birds call to one
another. Bees are already at work.
~WILLIAM LONGGOOD

Enjoying each other's good is
heaven begun.
~LUCY C. SMITH

Those who plant a garden work hand in hand with God.

Taking Time for Friends

How few take time for friendship! How few plan for it! It is treated as a haphazard, fortuitous thing. May good luck send us friends; we will not go after them. May favoring fortune bind our frienships: we will take no stitches ourselves. Review yesterday, and all your yesterdays. Did they open with any thought for friendship,—its pursuit, its retention, its glorification? Yet frienship requires painstaking. No art is so difficult, no craft so arduous. Roll a ball of clay and expect it to become a rose in your hand, but never expect an acquaintanceship, without care and thought, to blossom into frienship.

~AMOS R. WELLS

There is no use of living if our lives do not help other lives. They must help other lives if in themselves is the power of God.

~PHILLIPS BROOKS

A friend will strengthen you with her prayers, bless you with her love, and encourage you with her heart.

~ANTIQUE SAMPLER

Love is not getting, but giving; not a wild dream of pleasure, and a madness of desire—oh, no, love is not that,—it is goodness and honor, and peace and pure living—yes, love is that, and it is the best thing in the world, and the thing that lives longest.

~HENRY VAN DYKE

It is wonderful to think what the presence of one human being can do for another,—change everything in the world.

~GEORGE S. MERRIAM

Sunshine
and Flowers

Those who bring sunshine
to the lives of others
cannot keep it from
themselves.
JAMES M. BARRIE

© DEBBIE MUMM

Friends of the Earth

The very act of planting a seed in the earth has in it to me something beautiful. I always do it with a joy that is largely mixed with awe. I watch my garden beds after they are sown, and think how one of God's exquisite miracles is going on beneath the dark earth out of sight. I never forget my planted seeds. Often I wake in the night and think how the rains and the dews have reached to the dry shell and softened it, how the spirit of life begins to stir within, and the individuality of the plant to assert itself; how it is thrusting two hands forth from the imprisoning husk, one, the root, to grasp the earth, to hold itself firm and absorb its food, the other stretching above to find the light, that it may drink in the breeze and sunshine and so climb to its full perfection of beauty. It is curious that the leaf should so love the light and the root so hate it.

~Celia Thaxter

Nobody has ever measured, even poets, how much a heart can hold.

~Zelda Fitzgerald

Delight yourself in the Lord and he will give you the desires of your heart.

~Psalm 37:4

As for marigolds, poppies, hollyhocks, and valorous sunflowers, we shall never have a garden without them, both for their own sake, and for the sake of old-fashioned folks, who used to love them.

~Henry Ward Beecher

The art of being happy lies in the power of extracting happiness from common things.

~Henry Ward Beecher

Let us hope that sometime soon we may stop and make deliberate choice of a sweeter, quieter, friendlier life. By cutting down our social tasks and intellectual activities, let us make time for rest and home, and for remembrance of others whose houses and lives adjoin our own.

~Anonymous

Friendship, like love, must be largely taken "for better, for worse." It is idle to "throw over" a friend who in many ways gives you pleasant and agreeable companionship, because, you discover faults not at first perceived. If one waits to find perfection in his friend, he will probably wait long and die unfriended at last.

~Lilian Whiting

It pays to be happy. Happiness is not a luxury, but a necessity. The beneficial effect of mental sunshine on life, ability, strength, vitality, endurance, is most pronounced.

~Christina D. Larson

Happiness is a thing to be practiced, like the violin.

~John Lubbock

Happiness is cheap enough, yet how dearly we pay for its counterfiet.

~Anonymous

Cheerfulness is the atmosphere
in which all things thrive.

JEAN PAUL RICHTER

Recipe for a Friend

God made the perfect recipe
When He made you,
For all the right ingredients
Were sent from up above.
A dash of sweetness, pinch of fun,
A cup of love, then He was done.
He simply chose to bless me too,
By giving me a friend like you.

ANONYMOUS

Those who would make friends must cultivate the qualities which are admired and which are attractive to others. We must cultivate generosity and large-heartedness; we must be magnanimous and tolerant; we must look upward and be hopeful, cheery and optimistic. No one will be attracted by a gloomy pessimist. If you have friends, don't be afraid to express your friendship; don't be afraid to tell them you admire or love them. A woman was asked how she managed to get along so well with disagreeable people. "It is very simple," she replied; "all I do is try to make the most of their good qualities and pay no attention to their disagreeable ones." No better formula by which to win and hold friends can be found.

~Anonymous

There are friends who are to us like a great rock in a weary land. We flee to them in the heat of parching days and rest in their shadow. A friend in whom we can confide without fear of disappointment; who, we are sure, will never fail us, will never cease her love in serving us, who always has healing tenderness for the hurt of our heart, comfort for our sorrows, and cheer for our discouragement. Such a friend is not only a rock of shelter for us in time of danger but is also as rivers of water in a thirsty land, when our hearts cry out for life and love.

~J. R. M.

We gain life as we use what life we have, and we gain it as we are in sympathy, companionship, or accord with those who truly live.

~Edward Everett Hale

© DEBBIE MUMM

Afternoon Tea

"You can ask Diana to come over and spend the afternoon with you and have tea here."

"Oh, Marilla!" Anne clasped her hands. "How perfectly lovely! You are able to imagine things after all or else you'd never have understood how I've longed for that very thing. It will seem so nice and grown-uppish. No fear of my forgetting to put the tea to draw when I have company. Oh, Marilla, can I use the rosebud spray tea set?"

"No, indeed! The rosebud tea set! Well, what next? You know I never use that except for the minister or the ladies' society. You'll put down the old brown tea set. But you can open the little yellow crock of cherry preserves. It's time it was being used anyhow—I believe it's beginning to work. And you can cut some fruitcake and have some of the cookies and snaps."

"I can just imagine myself sitting down at the head of the table and pouring out the tea," said Anne, shutting her eyes ecstatically. "And asking Diana if she takes sugar! I know she doesn't but of course I'll ask her just as if I didn't know. And then pressing her to take another piece of fruitcake and another helping of preserves. Oh Marilla, it's a wonderful sensation just to think of it."

~L. M. MONTGOMERY

I am your servant! Everything I have is yours. But even as I say that, I know you are serving me more than I am serving you. At your command all the resources of heaven and earth are at my disposal, and even the angels help me.

~Thomas A Kempis

Above all else, guard your heart, for it is the wellspring of life.

~Proverbs 4:23

I do not lose patience with the birds, however sorely they try me. I love them too well. How should they know that the garden was not planted for them.

~Celia Thaxter

That little bird has chosen his shelter; above it are the stars and the deep heaven of worlds; yet he is rocking himself to sleep without caring for tomorrow's lodging, calmly clinging to his little twig and leaving God to think for him.

~Martin Luther

Little drops of water, little grains
    of sand,
Make the mighty ocean and the
    pleasant land.
Little deeds of kindness,
    little words of love,
Help to make earth happy like the
    heaven above.

~Julia A. Fletcher Carney

The best and most beautiful things in the world cannot be seen or even touched. They must be felt with the heart.

~Helen Keller